CONTENTS

WHAT IS A REPTILE?

How is a box turtle like a python? A crocodile like an iguana? A chameleon (kuh-**mee**-lee-uhn) like a lizard? All these animals are alike in one important way—they are reptiles.

My name's Camilla, and I'm a chameleon. Chameleons can change color. Meet some of my friends.

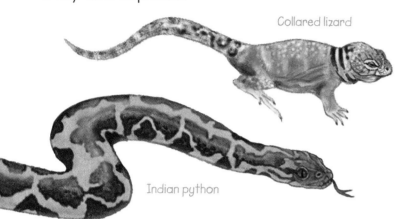

Collared lizard

Indian python

Nile crocodile

You can see that reptiles vary greatly in size, shape, and color. Like many animals, including humans, reptiles are **vertebrates**—animals with backbones. And like people, they use lungs to breathe.

Eastern box turtle

How Many Reptiles?

In this desert scene, all the animals are reptiles–except one. Circle the reptiles. Write the total number in the box.

number of reptiles _____
Which animal is NOT a reptile? Look carefully! _____

COOL WORD

A reptile's scales are made of **keratin**, the same as your fingernails.

Look Inside!

Look at the crocodile's backbone and lungs. Then find those parts on the garter snake. Write lungs and backbone on the lines.

Reptile skin is dry and rough. The skin of lizards and snakes is made of overlapping scales. The scales of turtles and crocodiles grow into hard, bony plates.

Many kinds of reptiles shed their skin, or **molt**, several times a year. New scales grow under the old ones, and the skin loosens and falls off. Snakes crawl out of their old skin and leave it behind in one piece. Lizard skin comes off in big strips.

Their skin keeps water in reptiles' bodies for a long time. That's why so many kinds of reptiles can live in deserts and other dry places.

Crocodile

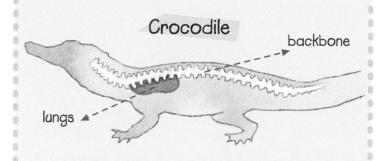

backbone

lungs

Garter Snake

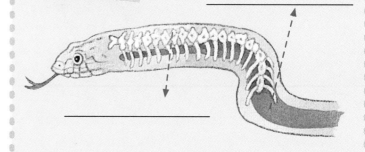

_____

_____

Reptiles are cold-blooded animals. That means they have no built-in way to control the temperature of their bodies. When their surroundings are cold, they are cold. When it's warm out, they are warm. To stay alive, cold-blooded animals must not become extremely hot or cold. That's why you might see a snake sunning itself on a rock on a cool day. But if the day turns hot, the snake will find a shady place to cool off.

Reptiles live almost everywhere in the world, usually on land. Here are two places you will find reptiles.

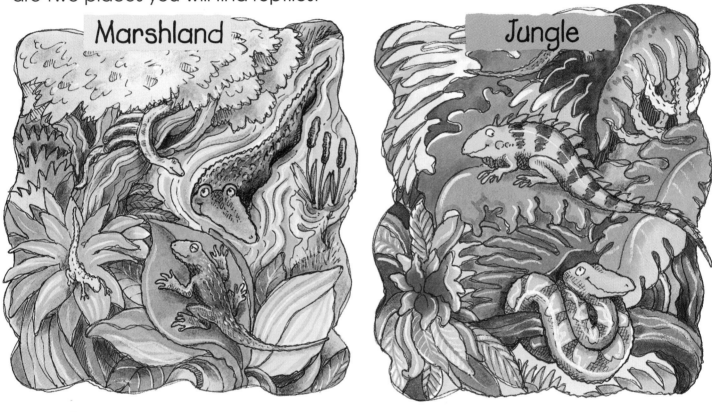

Marshland

Jungle

Reptile Code

Put a letter in place of each number to finish the sentence. Then answer the question.

c	t	a	t	r	i	n	A
1	2	3	4	5	6	7	8

Snakes can be found on all continents except _____.

8 7 4 3 5 1 4 6 1 3

Can you guess why?

Most reptiles can see well. The kinds of reptiles that are active at night have long, narrow pupils, which can open very wide to let in as much light as possible. Reptiles that stay active during the day and sleep at night have round pupils.

Many reptiles can hear low sounds. Snakes can't hear sounds, though. They "hear" by feeling vibrations that travel through the ground. Most reptiles eat other animals. Some lizards and turtles eat mainly plants. Reptiles can go without food for a long time.

stay safe, Snake!

Help the snake get away from its enemies.

Reptile Review

Complete the sentences with the words below. Then write the words in the puzzle.

lungs   temperature
land   reptiles
backbone   plates

My tongue is really long. It's coated with sticky stuff that helps me catch prey.

AWESOME!
There are more than 6,000 kinds of reptiles. Some are as tiny as two inches long. Others are longer than 30 feet.

Across

2. Reptiles breathe air through _____.

5. Cold-blooded animals do not have a constant body _____.

6. Most reptiles live on _____.

Down

1. Reptile skin is made of scales or bony _____.

3. An animal that is a vertebrate has a _____.

4. Turtles, snakes, lizards, and crocodiles are all _____.

LEAPIN' LIZARDS

The earliest lizards lived on Earth about 200 million years ago during the time of the dinosaurs, their reptile cousins. Lizards come in many colors and sizes. Most walk on four legs, but some don't have any legs at all.

Green iguana

Chilean cave lizard

Five-lined skink

Lizards defend themselves in unusual ways. Some have tails that break off when they are attacked. The tail wriggles around and distracts the attacker while the lizard escapes. Luckily, the tail grows back. Some lizards bluff. They puff up their bodies and hiss while lashing their tails. Some lizards change colors for protection.

Cracks in the lizard's backbone mark weak places where the tail can break apart.

Lizard Code

Put a letter in place of each number to finish the sentence.

r	t	o	i	G	m	l	a	e	n	s
1	2	3	4	5	6	7	8	9	10	11

The only poisonous lizard in the United States is the

☐ ☐ ☐ ☐ ☐ ☐ ☐ ☐ ☐ ☐ ☐ .
5 4 7 8 6 3 10 11 2 9 1

COOL WORD

Dinosaur means "terrible lizard." Unlike lizards, though, many dinosaurs walked on strong back legs.

Most lizards eat insects, slugs (snails without shells), and other small animals. The chameleon uses its long, sticky tongue to catch insects quicker than you can say *flick*!

Big lizards, such as Komodo dragons, eat pigs, deer, and other large animals. Some lizards, iguanas for example, are plant eaters.

AWESOME!
The world's biggest lizard, the Komodo dragon, can be as long as nine to ten feet and weigh nearly 300 pounds.

Puzzling Lizards

Complete the sentences with the words below. Then write the words in the puzzle.

slugs   iguana
dinosaurs   tails
tongue   four

Across

1. Lizards lived during the time of the _____.

4. Most lizards walk on _____ legs.

5. A chameleon catches bugs with its long, sticky _____.

Down

2. One lizard that eats plants is the _____.

3. Some lizards eat_____.

5. Some lizards drop their_____ when they're in trouble.

Lizards really get around! Some swim and some fly—well, almost. A group of lizards called flying dragons glides from tree to tree the same way flying squirrels do.

Draco lizard

Most lizards scamper about using their sharp claws to hold on to rough surfaces. One kind, the gecko, has slits on its toes that act like suction cups to help it stick to things. Geckos can walk upside down on a ceiling or a pane of glass!

Some lizards that live on the ground, such as skinks, have very weak legs—or no legs at all.

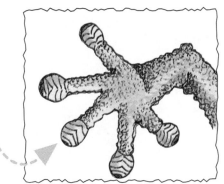

AWESOME!

How do you tell a legless lizard from a snake? Lizards have eyelids and ear openings. Snakes don't have either one.

Great plains skink

Guess the Lizard

Use the clues to write the names of the lizards.

flying dragon   iguana   gecko   skink   Komodo dragon

1. I'm a real heavyweight. _____

2. Maybe I look like one, but I'm no snake. _____

3. My toes are the stickiest. _____

4. Let's eat a salad. _____

5. I glide through the air with the greatest of ease. _____

Leapin' Lizards

SLITHERING SNAKES

W hat's the biggest difference between snakes and most other reptiles? Right! Snakes have no legs. Most slide along the ground by squeezing the muscles attached to their backbones so that their bodies make loops. The loops push on the ground or in the water, and the snakes move forward. Snakes can twist their long, thin bodies every which way, even into tight balls, to protect themselves from enemies.

Indian cobra

Corn snake

Ribbon snake

Horseshoe snake

Word Find

Circle four places where snakes can be found. Look ↑, ↗ and ↘.

ground water land trees

Z	T	I	K	Z	E	D
Q	S	R	A	R	E	N
D	D	R	E	L	R	U
E	N	T	H	E	V	O
L	A	F	R	N	S	R
W	L	O	Q	D	S	G

AWESOME!

Snakes that live in deserts move by resting on their heads and tails and lifting the middle part of their bodies off the ground and swinging them forward in an S-shape. This movement, called sidewinding, helps keep their bellies off the scorching hot sand.

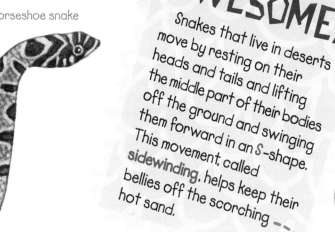

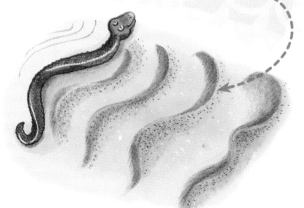

Snakes have a very good sense of smell that works in an unusual way. A snake's forked tongue flicks in and out constantly. This brings smells, such as the scent of animals to eat, or **prey**, into a special organ in the snake's mouth.

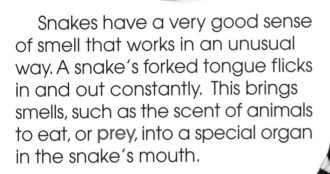

Viperine snake

Other organs in snakes' heads sense temperature. A snake moves its head from side to side to notice changes in the air temperature. The heat-sensing organ helps snakes find and strike warm-blooded prey in total darkness.

What's Long and Green?

One of the longest snakes is the common anaconda. It can grow as long as 30 feet! Look at the graph. About how many feet longer is the school bus than the anaconda? _____ How much longer is the anaconda than the alligator? _____

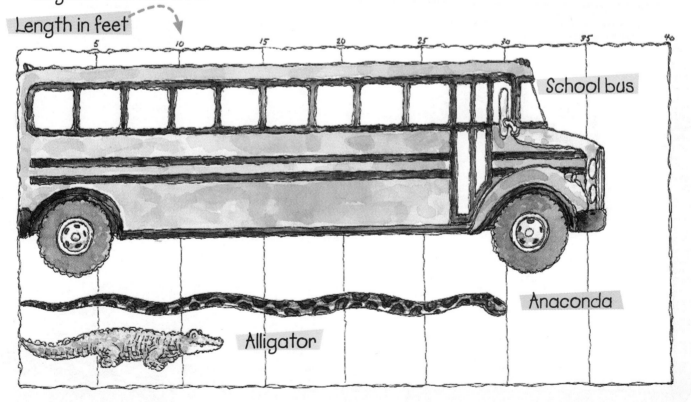

Length in feet

5   10   15   20   25   30   35   40

School bus

Anaconda

Alligator

Snakes defend themselves in various ways. Their patterns and colors help some snakes blend with their surroundings. Others have bright colors and patterns that warn enemies to stay away.

Many snakes make warning sounds, such as hissing or rattling. A few kinds of snakes puff up, or **inflate**, parts of their body to scare enemies. Some snakes shoot poison, or **venom**, from their fangs into their prey to kill it.

Northern copperhead

Eastern coral snake

Timber rattler

Others wrap themselves around their prey and squeeze the breath out of it.

Boa constrictor

AWESOME!

Most snakes lay eggs, sometimes as many as 100 at a time. A few kinds of snakes give birth to live young. Most newly hatched or born snakes are on their own—their mothers don't stay around to take care of them.

Small snakes eat mice and rats, fish, birds, eggs, and small reptiles. Big ones eat large animals, such as goats or even alligators. Most snakes swallow their prey whole. Their jaws unhinge so their mouths can expand enough to fit the food through. Snakes can go for as long as a year between meals.

You mean snakes eat lizards like me?

Snake Defenses

Match the defenses to the snakes.
Write the correct letters in the boxes.

A. warning sounds

B. warning colors

C. protective colors

D. changes in shape

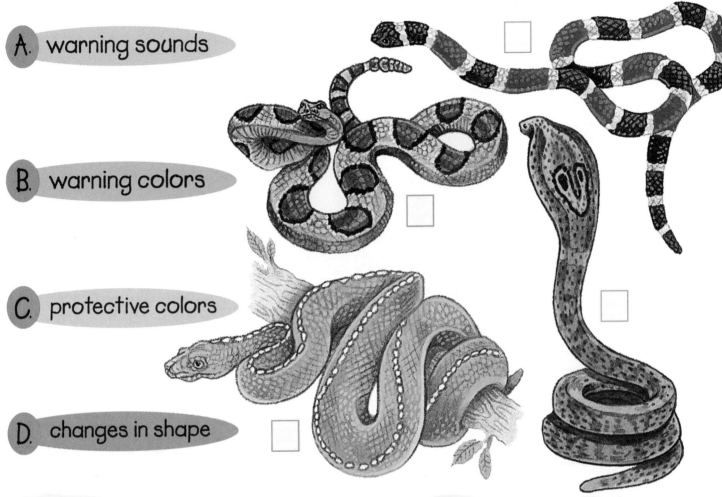

What's Wrong with the Sentences?

These sentences are false. Change a word in each one to make the sentence true.

1. The anaconda can grow as long as ten feet.

2. Most snakes take care of their babies.

3. Snakes that live in forests move by sidewinding.

4. Snakes use their fangs to sense smells.

TALK ABOUT TURTLES

Turtles are the only reptiles with shells. A turtle's shell is made of plates. The top plates, or scutes, are made of a material like your fingernails. The bottom plates are bony. The shell is part of the skeleton, so it can never be left behind. When in danger, a turtle pulls its head and legs into its shell for protection.

Spotted turtle

Some turtles live in water most of the time, but they breathe air. Most kinds of turtles eat plants and animals. Snapping turtles are fierce hunters with powerful jaws. They eat fish, frogs, salamanders, and even baby alligators.

Tortoises are turtles that live only on land. They eat plants. Gopher tortoises eat grasses and fruits.

write NOW!

Imagine that you carry your home around with you as a turtle does. What is your house like? Write a description.

All turtles and tortoises lay their eggs on land. Many female sea turtles bury their eggs on the same beach where they were hatched. When the eggs hatch, the babies run for the water. Most of the babies are eaten before they get to the ocean.

Turtle Race!

How many baby turtles do you see? _____

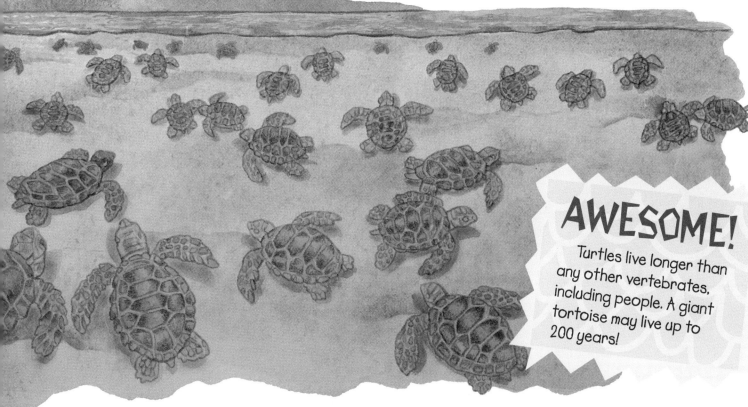

AWESOME!
Turtles live longer than any other vertebrates, including people. A giant tortoise may live up to 200 years!

You can tell whether a turtle lives mostly on land or in the water by the shape of its shell. Most land turtles, such as the side-necked turtle, have high domed shells. Water turtles, the painted turtle is one, have flatter shells.

Side-necked turtle   Painted turtle

Land or water?

Predict whether these turtles live in the water or on land by the shape of their shells. Write land or water on the line under each picture.

1. _____ 2. _____ 3. _____ 4. _____

CLEVER CROCODILES (ALLIGATORS, TOO)

You've probably seen crocodiles and alligators at a zoo or in pictures. Could you tell the crocodiles from the alligators? Their snouts and teeth are clues. A crocodile's snout is narrower than an alligator's, and it has a pair of bottom teeth that show when its mouth is shut. Both crocodiles and alligators live near water in warm parts of the world.

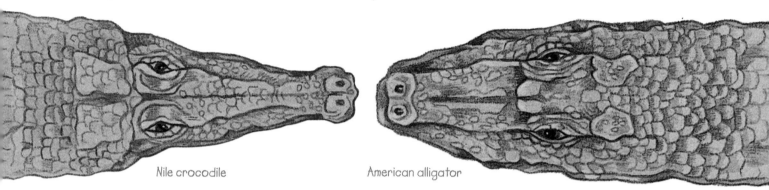

Nile crocodile

American alligator

Crocodiles and alligators have eyes, ears, and nostrils on top of their snout so they can hide themselves underwater as they hunt. Fast swimmers with strong jaws and big teeth, they eat just about any animal they can catch!

AWESOME!

Alligators in zoos have lived as long as 56 years. Crocodiles have lived up to 13-1/2 years. How much longer have alligators lived than crocodiles?

_____

What a grin!

Like most reptiles, crocodiles and alligators lay eggs. The mother alligator guards the eggs until they hatch and protects the young alligators for a year or more. Some crocodiles guard their nests, too.

The Nile crocodile guards her eggs. After the eggs hatch, she carries her babies gently in her mouth from their nest on land to the river. The young crocodiles stay with her for several weeks before they swim off on their own.

AWESOME!

Crocodiles cool off by resting with open mouths. They don't need to floss their teeth. Crocodiles let birds remove the food that's stuck in their teeth.

Get to the River

Help the mother Nile crocodile get her babies safely from their nest to the river.

REPTILE ROUNDUP

AWESOME!

The tuatara (too-uh-tar-uh) looks like a lizard but is actually the last of a large group of reptiles that lived before the dinosaurs. Tuataras can be found only in parts of New Zealand.

Reptile Search & Sort

Circle the reptile names in the puzzle. Then write the names of the reptiles where they belong in the chart.

anaconda   python   gecko
iguana
tortoise   chameleon
alligator   boa

O	I	R	T	B	O	A	E	T	E
C	A	L	L	I	G	A	T	O	R
H	Z	N	R	S	U	D	H	R	B
A	D	G	A	R	A	E	B	T	R
M	R	E	Q	C	N	R	S	O	L
E	L	C	S	N	O	E	M	I	N
L	N	K	C	O	N	N	A	S	H
E	H	O	M	E	L	E	D	E	D
O	K	P	Y	T	H	O	N	A	N
N	A	T	I	G	U	A	N	A	B

Crocodiles & Alligators

Snakes

Turtles & Tortoises

Lizards

WHAT IS AN AMPHIBIAN?

Toads, frogs, salamanders, and some other animals are amphibians (am-fib-ee-uhnz). These animals are cold-blooded, have backbones, and as adults most kinds breathe through lungs just as reptiles do. But amphibians have lived on Earth much longer than reptiles. Amphibians have skin without scales. They live part of their lives in the water and part on land.

Scientists have divided amphibians into three groups. Frogs and toads have four legs and no tail, salamanders have long tails and two or four legs, and caecilians (suh-sil-ee-uhnz) have no legs and look like large earthworms.

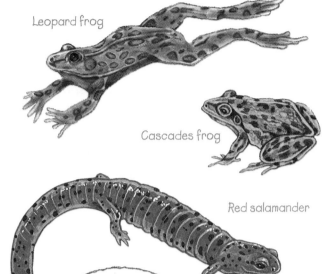

Leopard frog

Cascades frog

Red salamander

I'm Nando. That's short for Fernando Frog.

Caecilian

Lots of animals snack on amphibians. Help Nando escape from his enemies.

Nando Needs Help!

Alike and Different

Look at the circles with the words Amphibians and Reptiles. Write the letter for a way in which amphibians are different from reptiles under Amphibians. Write the letter for a way in which reptiles are different from amphibians under Reptiles. Where the circles overlap, write three letters for the qualities the animals share.

a. scaly skin

b. most breathe with lungs

c. skin without scales

d. vertebrates

e. cold-blooded

Amphibians   Reptiles

_____

_____   _____   _____

_____

AWESOME!
Like lizards and snakes, amphibians shed their skin as they grow. They usually eat the old skin.

COOL WORD
The word amphibia means "double life." In what way do amphibians lead a double life?

Most young amphibians, or larvae (lar-vee), begin their lives in the water. They breathe through gills as fish do. Have you ever seen a tadpole? Tadpoles are the larvae of frogs.

Over time, two weeks to several months, the larvae grow and change into adults that look very different from the larvae. Most adults leave the water and live on land.

> I started out as a tadpole, but now I hop around on land. Read about the parts of my life.

The Life of a Frog

Number the life stages of the frog in the right order.

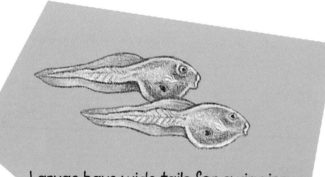

Larvae have wide tails for swimming.

Adult frogs live in and out of the water.

The tails of these larvae are shorter, and they breathe with lungs. Legs are growing and eyes are moving to the top of their heads. The larvae spend part of their time on land.

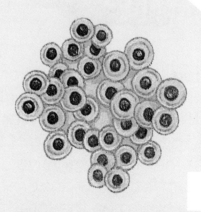

Eggs have gooey jelly around them instead of shells.

SHY SALAMANDERS

Salamanders are shy animals that usually come out only at night. They look like lizards, except their skin is moist and smooth and their heads are rounder.

Italian cave salamander

Crested newt

Olm

Salamanders that live in water all or most of their lives can breathe through their skin and with their gills and lungs. The mudpuppy's gills allow it to breathe oxygen dissolved in water.

AWESOME!

The name salamander comes from a word that means "fire animal." People once believed that salamanders were born from fire because they often came out of burning logs. Today we know that salamanders live in logs and crawl out when the logs burn.

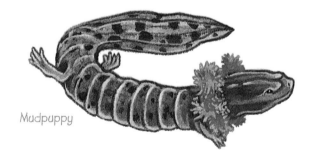
Mudpuppy

Salamanders that spend most or all of their lives on land may live under the ground, in rotting logs, under leaves, or even in trees. They must stay out of the sun to protect their moist, sensitive skin.

The adult spotted salamander spends most of its time hiding on the forest floor. At night, it hunts worms and insects. It grows to be about nine inches long.

Spotted salamander

Why do you think salamanders hunt for food at night?

_____

_____

_____

Salamander Code

Help! I just lost a leg. What should I do?
Use the code to answer the question.

a	o	n	G	w	r	t	e	h
▲	✳	❖	■	◎	✺	★	◉	✤

■ ✺ ✳ ◎   ▲ ❖ ✺ ★ ✤ ◎ ✺   ✳ ❖ ◎ !

Would a Salamander Live Here?

Draw salamanders in the places they could live.

FANTASTIC FROGS

European green tree frog

There are almost 4,000 different kinds of frogs, and they live in every part of the world except the frozen Antarctic. Frogs have smooth, moist skin the same as salamanders do, but their bodies are very different. Frogs have long, strong back legs for jumping.

Ornated horned frog

Common bullfrog

River frog

Froggy Math

1. The biggest frog is the Goliath frog of Africa. It is about one foot, or 12 inches, long. The smallest kinds are only about 1/2 inch long. How much longer is the biggest frog than the smallest?

_____

2. Many frogs can leap 20 times the length of their bodies. If a person four feet tall could do that, how far could the person jump?

_____

Gliding frog

3. The gliding frog uses its webbed feet to "fly" 50 feet through the air. How much longer is that than a 30-foot anaconda?

_____

Most frogs' eyes are large. They are set at the side of the head so the frogs can watch all around for danger. Some frogs' skins have bright colors to warn enemies to stay away.

Most frogs have colors and patterns that match their surroundings. This camouflage (kam-uh-flahzh) helps them hide from animals that want to eat them. Here's one example. The Asian leaf frog lives on forest floors. Its brown-and-yellow coloring and flat, pointy body make it look like a dead leaf.

Asian leaf frog

Hide and Seek

How many frogs can you find in this picture? Circle them.

HOP ALONG TOADS

Toads look quite a bit like frogs, but they are different in some ways. Toads have dry, bumpy skin, not smooth, moist skin. They have plumper bodies and shorter back legs than frogs do. Because their legs are short, they can't leap like frogs. Instead, most toads hop.

Midwife toad

Yosemite toad

AWESOME!
Some people believe that if you touch a toad you'll get warts. You don't have to be a toad expert to know that isn't true!

Giant toad

Green toad

Toads grow up in water, but most kinds spend much of their lives on land. Even land toads must keep their bodies from getting too dry. The spadefoot toad lives in hot, dry places. It keeps from drying out by burrowing underground. It may stay below the ground for months without eating. After a rainfall, it comes up at night and hunts for food.

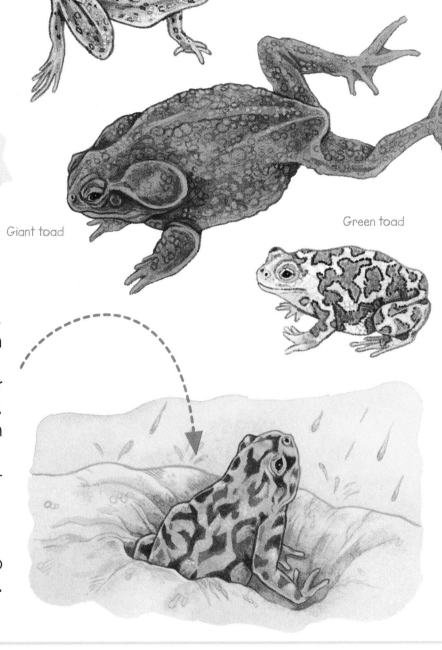

Great plains toad

Some male toads can puff up their throats to make noises that sound like flutes. Female toads can't do this.

Like frogs, many toads have long, sticky tongues that they use to catch worms, insects, and other small animals.

Toad or Frog?

Draw a line from each description to the correct animal. Then write **toad** and **frog** on the lines.

smooth and moist

short

plump

hop

dry and bumpy

long

leap

thin

_____

_____

AMPHIBIAN FUN

Name That Amphibian

Decide which kind of amphibian is talking. Write its name.

salamander   frog   toad

I think hopping is more dignified than leaping.

1. ___

I'm shy. People used to think I came from fire.

2. ___

I can jump higher than anybody!

3. ___

Fact or Fiction?

Write true or false after each sentence.

1. Frogs have smooth, moist skin.

2. Most salamanders come out at night.

3. Toads are better jumpers than frogs.

4. Some salamanders live in water.

5. Many frogs have bulging eyes to help them hide.

Write Now!

In one fairy tale, a princess kisses a frog and turns him into a prince. Make up your own amphibian fairy tale.

THE FUTURE OF REPTILES AND AMPHIBIANS

Although reptiles and amphibians have been around for millions of years, in many parts of the world they may not last much longer. Some reptiles and amphibians have already become extinct, or died off. These animals will never be seen again.

Here are some of the problems that threaten reptiles and amphibians.

- Air and water pollution caused by people is very harmful to these animals.

- Many reptiles and amphibians have lost their homes because people have built roads and houses where the animals live.

- Many reptiles and amphibians are taken from their wild homes to be sold. Animals such as snakes, turtles, and salamanders usually die when they are kept as pets.

Action Plan

Make a plan to help reptiles and amphibians. Write three ideas or steps of your plan.

_____

_____

_____

AWESOME!

The International Union for Conservation of Nature is working to make conditions better for amphibians all over the world. Write them to learn how you can help.

IUCN Species Survival Commision,
c/o Chicago Zoological Society,
Brookfield, IL 60503

MORE ABOUT REPTILES AND AMPHIBIANS

Books

Reptiles and Amphibians
   by Catherine Herbert Howell
What Is a Reptile?
   by Robert Snedden
Salamanders by Cherie Winner
Scaly Babies: Reptiles Growing Up
   by Ginny Johnston and Judy Cutchins
Slippery Babies: Young Frogs, Toads,
and Salamanders
   by Ginny Johnston and Judy Cutchins
Lizards by Claudia Schneiper
Amazing Crocodiles and Reptiles
   by Mary Ling
Amazing Snakes by Alexandra Parsons
Amazing Lizards by Trevor Smith

Internet Resources & CD-ROMs

Bill's Wildlife Links
   http://cccweb.com/wildlife.html
The World of Reptiles
   http://www.remedia.com
Froggy Page
   http://www.frog.simplenet.com

Video & Audio

Reptile
   eyewitness video produced
   by Dorling Kindersley
My Best Friend Is a Salamander
   audio cassette by Peter
   Himmelman, Baby Music Boom

ANSWERS

Page 2
Total # of reptiles: 12
The girl is not a reptile.

Page 5

Page 8

Crossword:
- 1 down / 1 across: **d i n o s a u r s** (1-across spelling "dinosaurs" with 3-s)
- **i g u a n a** (down)
- **f o u r** (4-across)
- **t o n g u e** (5-across)
- **t a i l s** (down)
- **s l u g s** (down)

Page 15
35

1. land
2. water
3. land
4. water

Page 16
42-1/2 years

Page 3

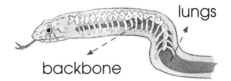

lungs

backbone

Page 6

Crossword:
- 1 down: **p** (palates)
- 2 across: **l u n g s**
- 3 down: **b a c k b o n e**
- 4 down: **r e p t i l e s**
- 5 across: **t e m p e r a t u r e**
- 6 across: **l a n d**

Page 10

Z	T	I	K	Z	E	D
Q	S	R	A	R	E	N
D	D	R	E	L	R	U
E	N	T	H	E	V	O
L	A	F	R	N	S	R
W	L	O	Q	D	S	G

Page 4
Antarctica
Most children will guess
that Antarctica is too
cold for reptiles.

Page 7
Gila monster

Page 9
1. Komodo dragon
2. skink
3. gecko
4. iguana
5. flying dragon

Page 11
About 6 feet
About 18 feet

Page 13

1. The anaconda can grow
   as long as 30 feet.
2. Most snakes don't take
   care of their babies.
3. Snakes that live in deserts
   move by sidewinding.
4. Snakes use their tongues
   to sense smells.

ANSWERS

Page 17

Page 18

O	I	R	T	B	O	A	E	T	E
C	A	L	L	I	G	A	T	O	R
H	Z	N	R	S	U	D	H	R	B
A	D	G	A	R	A	E	B	T	R
M	R	E	Q	C	N	R	S	O	L
E	L	C	S	N	O	E	M	I	N
L	N	K	C	O	N	N	A	S	H
E	H	O	M	E	L	E	D	E	D
O	K	P	Y	T	H	O	N	A	N
N	A	T	I	G	U	A	N	A	B

Crocodiles & Alligators
alligator

Snakes
anaconda
boa
python

Turtles & Tortoises
tortoise

Lizards
gecko
chameleon
iguana

Page 19

Page 20

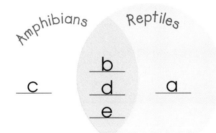

Amphibians: c, b, d, e
Reptiles: b, d, e, a

Page 21

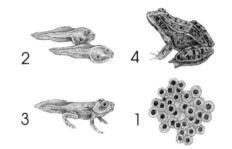

2, 4, 3, 1

Page 22
Most children will write that salamanders hunt at night to avoid the sun.

Page 23
Grow another one!

Children should draw salamanders in each of the environments except the desert.

Page 24
1. 11-1/2 inches
2. 80 feet
3. 20 feet

Page 25

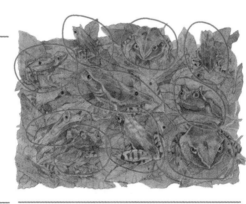

Page 27

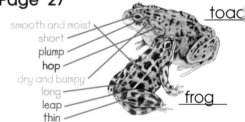

smooth and moist
short
plump
hop
dry and bumpy
long
leap
thin

toad

frog

Page 28
1. toad
2. salamander
3. frog

1. true
2. true
3. false
4. true
5. false